I Write to Breathe

By

Lora L. Mitchell

Lady L. Publishing
Copyright © 2025

Copyright © 2025 by Lora L. Mitchell

All rights reserved. Except as permitted under the U.S. Copyright Act of 1976, no part of this publication may be reproduced, distributed, or transmitted in any form or by any means, or stored in a database or retrieval system, without the prior written permission of the publisher

ISBN: 978-0-9976786-3-5

Website: www.loramitchellthewriter.com
Email: loramitchellthewriter@gmail.com

Like on Facebook at:
I Write To Breathe -
https://www.facebook.com/profile.php
Lora Mitchell Author

Follow on Instagram at
DiaryOfABlackGirlTheBook

Subscribe to the Author's Substack at
https://loramitchellthewriter.substack.com/

Support on Patreon at
https://www.patreon.com/c/LoraMitchellTheWriter

Acknowledgements

This has been a journey that has been filled with joy, sorrow, fun, heartbreak, and growth. I can't believe I am finally putting this book out. There are a few people I would like to thank for walking with me through this journey. First my parents, sister, and family. My family has walked with me through this writing journey for many years now. They make space for me to have writing time, support my books, and give ideas and ways to help make the process easier. I love that they love me, but also support my gift and joy of writing.

I also thank my friends for being a great support. Whether that means listening to me talk about my projects ad nauseum, reading snippets and ideas that I have, asking me how writing is going to keep me focused on my goals, or supporting writing events and launches I have had over the years, I am grateful for them.

I would next like to thank and pay tribute to those who have gone before me in this journey. I won't do a long list, though unfortunately the list could definitely be long. I will only list three people who have made such a huge impact in my life during the all too quick time our lives crossed.

Zu
Joseph Harris
Uncle L.C.

I have never met someone who loved words more than Zu. She was a writer's writer. She could write whole books in a matter of weeks. She loved the art of writing, the process of writing and editing, encouraging other writers, and teaching. I miss her everyday, especially as I try to write without her here. She would have loved this book and supported most of the things I have written.

Joseph was one of my oldest friends I made as an adult. From the day we met to the day he passed away, I didn't know adulthood without him. He was also a supporter of my dream and had plans of writing his own book. I miss him so much and think about what he would have thought of my life now. No matter what I know he would have been cheering me on and happy that I took the leap.

My Uncle L.C. left us in August of this year. I got to know him more closely the last couple of years and I was amazed by his love for family and me in particular. He enjoyed my stories about my students, my love for politics/activism, and my silliness from time to time. He also just wanted me to be safe and I am still touched by his protective instincts for our family and world. I miss him, especially his smile.

And before I forget, I would like to thank each and everyone of you who picked up this book. Thank you for choosing to read these words. If you are a writer, I hope this encourages you to keep going. Writing can be such a daunting, lonely, and anxiety-inducing process. Especially if you don't have people, including other writers, to encourage you. If that is you, this is your sign that you are meant to be a writer, your stories/words matter, and yes writing can feel like wrestling a bear, but the fight is worth it.

Thank you for sharing your words with the world, even if the only person in the world who ever sees them is you.

Thank You!!!!!!!!

Table of Contents

In Quiet Spaces	9
What A Way to Drown	11
Remember	14
I Can Hear	16
To Love	18
Embattled With the Muses	19
This Too Shall Pass	21
Ode to Writing	23
Blank Page	25
Ruth-Ann	27
Escape At the Desk	28
Anxiety, My Friend	31
Trust the Journey	35

Have You Seen Her?	37
Every Day	38
I Love Notebooks	39
When I Go Through Dry Writing Spells	41

In quiet spaces

In quiet spaces, I find
Safety
Corners and bathrooms,
Libraries and Cathedrals
Places where
Stillness
Privacy
And a little bit of mystery
Are still valued
And expected

In quiet spaces, I find
Danger
Ripping and running
Through pages of a book
I struggle to keep quiet
As paper turns into lands unknown
Ink into heroes, villains, and testimonies
Periods provide the beginning of knowledge
Exclamation points, the end of questions
My heart races
As quietness surrounds me
And the trains in my head
Are only matched in speed

By the temporary pause
Of the world around me.

In quiet spaces, I find
My cut partner and my friend.
Keeper of my most precious secrets
She betrays me, letting me know
They can't stay my own.
Writing in her brings great
Revelation
Excitement
Reflection
Questions
Art
We wrestle with thoughts
Great and little
Contradictions and analysis of my humanity
Are always on the table
As topics of discussion
Because between she and I
Quiet spaces only provide
The space
To pass the time.

What A Way to Drown

Laughter
Sib Talk
Commentary
Space

It feels good
As I let the water
Of the Place
Enter My Lungs

I enjoy and hear
Familiar voices flood my ears
Familiar faces fill my screens
Familiar presence fills my heart

Yet with each day
I feel me losing
Me.

I haven't written in months
I haven't listened to the music
Of my heart
Old friends wonder if I'm still alive
Family members are curious about

These people I talk to daily.

They've held me when I've been
Broken
Corrected my flaws
Welcomed me in when I felt like
An other
And helped me push
Dark clouds away.

While this baptism has been
Beautiful
It's time to come back up.
It's time to find me again.
It's time to remember who I am
It's time to resuscitate
The spirit in me
That has been taking in water
Instead of flying free.

So as I sore to the top
I remember my journey from before
And the
Laughter
Sib Talk
Commentary

Space
That made losing myself
A beautiful way to drown.

Remember

Promise me you'll remember to be yourself
Against the world's mission to
Change you
Rearrange you
Contort you
Abort you
Never give in to what isn't authentically
You

Promise me you'll remember to grow
Always be learning
Always be in wonder
Always seek to expand your horizons
Never miss the opportunity to experience all
that life has to offer
You

Promise me you'll remember to forgive
yourself
To be human is to be
Flawed
To forgive is
Divine
Forgiveness allows you to heal

Grow
Move on
Teach
Your past wrongs are a part of the tapestry
That produces a wiser, better
You.

I Can Hear

The only sounds I can hear are
Tick Tock
Tick Tock
Tick Tock
And the thoughts in my head.

"Can I really write something worth reading?"
"Is it worth it?"
"Am I wasting my time"
"You know it took _____ (insert famous author here) 30 years to write his/her/their first book."

Doubts and faith begin to fill the air.
Nervousness and confidence fight for
Who will win this war?

All of the items in my room
Stare at me with bated breath
(Okay, maybe not breath since their inanimate)
Hoping in anticipation
That I will

Pick up that pen
And write.

To Love

To love is to lose.
Yet, to love is to gain.

To love is to fear.
Yet, to love is to find courage.

To love is to hurt.
Yet, love heals in ways unknown.

In times of tragedy, crisis, and separation
love feels like a betrayal.
Yet it's the only thing that brings you back to life.

Embattled With the Muses

Tick Tock
Tick Tock
Tick Tock
Goes the clock
As I sit at this computer.

Words need to appear during this
Writing hour.
What actually appears?
My frustrations.
My insecurities.
My fears and failures.

Click Clack
Click Clack
Click Clack
Goes my pen
As I play with the top.

"Did Hemingway go through this?"
"Was Toni Morrison this worried about putting words on a page?"
"There's no way Maya Angelou had this much issue writing, right?"

None of these thoughts
Help me
Put words on the page.

They do remind me
I'm part of a legacy
Of a long list of creatives
Tasked with wrestling the muses
For the words to come to life.

This Too Shall Pass

Sitting around the family table,
I found peace,
Grace,
Love.

Learning to start afresh
These roots helped
Ground me
In the reality
Of who I am.

Others came before me
Others are coming after me
They have survived
Many winters before this one.
I will make it to spring.

Ancestors
Elders
Younguns
Kin
Chosen and Blood
All made with love
Tap my ears

Flood my heart
Open my mind
To the awareness
That I belong
To something
Bigger
Greater
Stronger
Than this moment

And just like
The trees
And flowers
That surround me
I too
Will spring
To life
Again.

Ode to Writing

True love awaits in the gentle breezes of these pages.
It's holy, righteous, sexy, murderous,
Angry, sad, gleeful, full of pleasure,
Full of sorrow.
It's you!

My mind wakes up wanting to fill you,
Touch you,
Hold you,
Write for you.

For you are my safe place
My dangerous liaison
My cut partner and friend.
Holder of my most dangerous secrets.
Revealer of my most intimate truths.

You speak to me.
Turning over and over again in my heart
Until I let you go
Free.
To move about the world in ways I can't anticipate.
Hearing you gives life to me.

For I am in awe of being your author and audience.

To writing,
My greatest gift, enemy, and friend.

This is my ode to you.

Blank Page

The scariest place
The most exhilarating space
The alpha of greatness
The omega of innocence

The blank page
Leaves me open
To the possibilities
Of what's ahead.

It also reminds me
That the future
Is all on me.

The words
Decisions
Actions
I choose from
Are all my own

Whatever they become
Whatever I become
It's up to me.

The blank page
A powerful metaphor
For each new day
Gives me an opportunity
To start anew

The rest is up to me.

Ruth-Ann

Ruth-Ann puts the door on the house
Next to the plant under the window
Staring
Hoping that it turns out right.
Her hands ache
As she glues the doorknob on
With painstaking
Concentration and clarity
Gold knob on the blue door
With the red window seats
Reminding her of home
Placing the window pane in its place
She tries to forget
That she hasn't seen her daughter in months
With her focus,
She puts away the distraction of
Grandkids who no longer call.
She just looks through the window
At the mother and father
Who were once there
For her.

Escape at the Desk

Books
Pens
Erasers
Pencils
Sharpeners
Staplers
Push pins
Clips

It seems like I'm always preparing to write, draw, or organize something.

For someone with so much stuff,
You'd think I'd written the Great American novel by now.
Nope!

Drawers full of papers
Pens
Paper clips
Binders
Invite me
To dance with them
Create with them

Set the world on fire
With them

Books
Written by those
Who've left their marks
On the world
Scream to me
"Read me!"
They say.
"Let me tell you how the world came to be.
Let me help you escape how it is."

Erasers
Remind me that anything can be fixed.
Mistakes happen
You can start anew

Pencils and sharpeners
Dare me to try
Try something new
Try something bold
Try to create
Knowing with every mark
You too, make your mark
On the world.

Staplers
Push pins
Paper clips
Remind me that there's structure to it all.
All of the creative mess
Makes sense
And can come together
To make a tapestry of the heart.

Anxiety My Friend

Anxiety, my friend
We have a love-hate relationship
You can sometimes dominate my life and mind
In ways
That make me want to extricate you
Completely from my life.

The fears
The stories
The screams
The quiet whispers

They all worry me.
My worries worry me
And I feel crazy.

Anxiety, my friend
I rail against you,
But truth be told
You also illuminate
My deepest fears
My darkest spaces
My terrifying back room.

You challenge me
To face
My deepest fears
My darkest spaces
My terrifying back room.

Without you
I think I would
Pretend they don't exist
That they don't matter
That I don't matter

Without you
Would I be as attuned
To what needs to be addressed
To what needs to be faced
To what needs to be?

My fears
Point me to what concerns me.
They force me to consider
What's real?
What isn't?
How do I feel?

My dark spaces
Need light.
They need to be seen.
They need to be faced.
They need to be.

My dark room
Needs to be illuminated.
I need to realize
What's in there
Isn't so scary after all
It just is
Another part of me
A part of who I am.

Thank you, anxiety.
While I won't exalt you
Higher than I ought to
I will
Appreciate
Your space
In my life
And give myself
Grace
For when you show up.

Until next time,
Goodbye
Anxiety, my friend.

Trust the Journey

Trust that God has you
And that you will be fine.
Through every storm
Through every joy
Through every day.

Trust that life is worth waking up for each day.
Even the worst days are blessed by beauty.
The greatest make life worth living
The mundane reminds us that
Like the heartbeat,
Life keeps beating
And there's more on the other side of the day.

Trust that people are kind
Good
Worthy of love
Yes, even them.
We all have the capacity for good.
The capacity to enrich each other.
The capacity to make each day easier
Brighter

Better.

Trust that our shared humanity is key
To our survival
To our thriving
To us finding the solutions we desperately need.

Have You Seen Her?

Have you seen her?
There she is!

Pigtails flowing in the wind
As she walks down the street
Lost in the music
Of the headphones
In her ear.

She smiles
Flowing through life.
She is beautiful.
Eyes shining
Bursts of light
Noticing the little people
She meets.

Her hands are in her pockets
Fingering whatever
Mysteries lie within.
She breathes the sun
She walks with pride
She makes me want to know her.
She is me.

Every Day

Every step leads to the next step
Every day leads to the next day
Every moment leads to the next moment

It's only when you look back that you realize
how significant those
Steps
Days
Moments
Were
And how
They Add Up.

In the present
They are just called
Life.

Live your life.

I Love Notebooks

I love notebooks!

The designs on the outside. The crackle the newly opened pages make.

The slight adjustments it makes for whatever changes and insertions you include in it.

Bookmarks!
Pens!
Programs!

As long as it's small enough, it can fit.

I love the feel of each page under my fingers. That tactile sense of grounding. That knowing that:

Creation happens here.

What once was not, becomes:

At the stroke of a pen.
At the mark of a pencil.

At the movement of a hand.

Moving your body to get the right position,
To write.

It feels good.
It feels real.
It feels like breathing.

I love notebooks,
And I'm glad I get to write in one
Right now!

When I Go Through Dry Writing Spells

When I go through dry writing spells,

I miss words. I miss stories.

I miss putting my pen to paper or typing on my keyboard.

I miss the characters and headspace.

And that longing causes me to try again, where they meet me with open arms and say,

"We're still here."

42

Author's Note

I would like to thank you for reading this book. It is truly a love letter to all of the writers and creators out there that wake up everyday seeking to make, polish, and share their art with others. You are the reason someone has a smile on their face, a tear from the heart, are able to think in ways that were once foreign, gain empathy for others around the world, and are able to feel in a world that is more and more trying to get us to numb ourselves. Thank you!

If you would like to book me for an event, speaking engagement, or to be a guest on your show, feel free to email me at loramitchellthewriter@gmail.com.

Subscribe to my Substack at
https://loramitchellthewriter.substack.com

www.ingramcontent.com/pod-product-compliance
Lightning Source LLC
LaVergne TN
LVHW041502070426
835507LV00009B/755